Castles, Houses and Gardens of Scotland

Castles, Houses and Gardens of Scotland

by

Nan Pattullo

William Blackwood & Sons Ltd
Edinburgh and London

Printed and bound by
L. van Leer & Co. N.V. Amsterdam

Contents

List of Illustrations

Foreword

by The Rt. Hon. Earl Cawdor, T.D., F.S.A., F.S.A.Scot., Chairman of the Historic Buildings for Scotland.

In Scotland we are fortunate in the possession of McGibbon and Ross, "The Castellated and Domestic Architecture of Scotland", in five priceless volumes, now long out of print and very hard to come by. This work is very comprehensive, but the information having been collected eighty to ninety years ago, is not entirely up to date. Much has been discovered in the intervening years, especially painted ceilings during the past two decades or so. Charming as are the drawings by McGibbon and Ross, they are not in colour.

The intelligent interest in good houses seems to have increased in recent years due probably to the greater mobility available to-day. At all events there is no lack of books on the subject, mostly dealing with the technical aspect, but all as far as I know, illustrated by photographs or drawings.

This book, by Miss Pattullo, breaks new ground; it deals with exteriors and interiors of Castles and Houses all over Scotland and includes gardens in many cases. It is unusual in that it is illustrated by coloured photographs. Miss Pattullo is an admirable photographer, and as I know, has taken an immense amount of trouble both with her text and with her illustrations.

The book is the outcome of many years of hard work and it will, I hope, make a wide appeal to people possessing different interests.

Introduction

When I was lecturing in America on Scottish castles and houses my audiences kept asking for my photographs in book form. The idea of a book had not previously occurred to me, the photographs having been taken for use as colour slides, but this book is the outcome of years of work on this record in photographs of Scottish castles and houses up to the late seventeenth century.

These houses were built to last, and with some changes, are still in use as homes. At the same time I have tried to show a few of the many treasures still to be found in these homes, most of which have come down through the years as family heirlooms. Months have been spent in trying to verify the information in the texts as I do not profess to be an expert on architecture, china, embroidery, tapestry, period furniture and art.

Books consulted include the following:

The Castellated and Domestic Architecture of Scotland, McGibbon and Ross (1887-92)
Scottish Castles, W. Douglas Simpson (1959)
The Scottish Castle, Stewart Cruden (1960)
The Fortified House in Scotland, Nigel Tranter (1962-)
The Stones of Scotland, G. Scott-Moncreiff (1938)
Scotland in the Middle Ages, Cosmo Innes (1860)
The Ancient Stones of Scotland, W. Douglas Simpson (*1965*)
The Lothians, Ian Finlay (*1960*)
The Scots Gard'ner, John Reid 1683 (reprinted 1907)
Scottish Pageant, Agnes Mure Mackenzie (1946)

In this connection I would like to acknowledge with gratitude the help I have received from the staffs of the Scottish Record Office, the Royal Commission on the Ancient and Historical Monuments of Scotland, the Royal Scottish Musuem, the Edinburgh Public Libraries, and not least, the owners of the various properties, many of whom were extremely kind and hospitable.

My special thanks are due to Miss Catherine Cruft of the Scottish National Monuments Record for having checked all the architectural texts before they were printed, and to Earl Cawdor and Professor Donaldson for their practical encouragement.

Many of the photographs have already been taken for a second book, which would include later Scottish houses designed by Sir William Bruce and the members of the famous Adam family of architects, if this book is well received.

The photograph of the personal Coat-of-Arms of Her Majesty Queen Elizabeth, the Queen Mother, has been kindly lent by the Edinburgh Tapestry Company, and that of Rory Mor's horn at Dunvegan by the Royal Scottish Museum. With those two exceptions all the photographs in the book have been taken by myself.

Some of the houses are regularly open to the public, and in many other cases they can be visited by appointment. A handbook, giving details of garden openings, is published by Scotland's Garden Scheme, 26 Castle Terrace Edinburgh, price 2/6.

Edinburgh
1967.

N . PATTULLO

Eilandonan Castle, in Wester Ross, an ancient stronghold of the Mackenzies and the Macraes, looking across to the Isle of Skye.

Eilandonan Castle stands in a commanding position on a rocky island at the junction of three sea lochs. A vitrified fort on this site was replaced in the 13th century by a castle with a great wall of enceinte.

Mackenzie, Chief of Kintail, was given custody of this castle, and finally possession, as a reward for his help in defeating the Vikings at the Battle of Largs in 1263, and we find him living there in 1267. For a long time before this the Mackenzies had been in this area as "frontiersmen" to protect this part of the coast from invasion.

In the 14th century the castle was in the hands of Randolph, Earl of Moray but in the 15th and 16th centuries Eilandonan was the great western castle of the Mackenzies whose territory extended right across Scotland from coast to coast. Eilandonan was often garrisoned for the Mackenzie Chiefs by the Macraes who were usually the Hereditary Constables known as Mackenzie's Coat of Mail.

In 1719 Eilandonan was destroyed by gunfire from three English warships but was rebuilt by Col. Macrae-Gilstrap this century.

The keep is probably 14th century and its north and east walls seem to have been raised upon the older wall of enceinte, with walls 10 feet thick. There is an early type of water cistern, probably fed by a spring, which is connected to the courtyard by a long narrow passage with walls about five feet thick and probably originally about fifteen feet high.

Traquair House, Peebles shire, showing the early tower framed in the gateway.

The early tower shown on the left of the picture was remodelled by Sir William Stuart, 5th Laird of Traquair in 1599, and the initials S.W.S. and the date 1599 carved above one window commemorate this. In the tower itself there are remains of murals dating from about 1550.

The extension on the right was added later, and here the central dormer window is dated 1642. The low wings forming the sides of the courtyard and the fine wrought-iron gateway were added in 1695 and working drawings with this date still exist.

Traquair House, Peeblesshire. Said to be the oldest inhabited house in Scotland.

Traquair House, the home of P. Maxwell Stuart Esq., has remained unaltered since the 17th century. In early times this was a Royal demesne, and the earliest recorded royal visit to Traquair is that of Alexander I in 1107 when Traquair was a hunting-lodge on the edge of Ettrick Forest.

During the centuries 27 Scottish and English kings have been sheltered by Traquair, including Mary, Queen of Scots, who stayed there with her husband Darnley in 1566.

There are Royal Charters given at Traquair and signed by King David I in 1133 and 1142, and it was at Traquair in 1175 that King William the Lion signed the charter granting permission for the hamlet of Glasgow to be elevated to the status of a Bishop's Burgh. Glasgow's present population is about a million.

Traquair is open to the public on most afternoons during the summer.

The drawing-room at Traquair House.

Until 1954 the panelling in the drawing-room at Traquair was covered by a heavy flock wallpaper, but the 18th century panelling has now been restored to its original beauty.

A harpsichord made by Andreas Ruchers in 1641 is shown in the centre of the room, and on the table in the foreground is a fine collection of Jacobite wine glasses, for the Stuart family were ardent Jacobites.

The King's Room, Traquair, with Mary, Queen of Scots' bed.

Mary, Queen of Scots' bed in the King's Room at Traquair was brought here from Terregles, a Maxwell property in the west of Scotland. The appliqué work is the original but the silk backing has been renewed in the same golden colour.

This is the room occupied by Mary and her husband Darnley when they stayed at Traquair in 1566. The oak cradle used for her son James VI of Scotland and I of England can be seen in the drawing-room.

In the thickness of the walls there is a secret stair from this room and from the Priest's Room above.

An unused embroidered panel, height 33½ ins., width 26½ ins., coloured worsted on linen canvas, circa 1600.

This embroidered panel, worked in fine tent stitch, is one of several at Traquair. The motifs of birds, beasts and fruits were for cutting out for appliqué work, and the Traquair panels, all different in design, had not been cut but laid away in safe storage, which probably accounts for the freshness of the colours. One illustration of their use can be seen at Lennoxlove, applied to a wall covering of 18th century silk damask.

This charming bedroom was once the monks' dormitory.

The early house at Windy Hills, with its five foot thick stone walls, is still the core of the present house of Milton Brodie, although of course it has been added to through the centuries. The thickness of the walls can be seen at the window as this charming bedroom is in the oldest part of the house and is thought to have been the Monks' dormitory.

The garden of Milton Brodie was made by Cistercian monks in the 13th century

King David I invited the Abbey of Melrose to send a band of monks to build an Abbey in the Laigh of Moray, and the king himself stayed nearby in 1151 while engaged upon the foundation of Kinloss Abbey.

The Cistercians were gardeners, builders, masons and herbalists, and later on when one of their number was appointed a member of the Chapter of Elgin Cathedral he was called the Chanter of Moray, and the Abbey of Kinloss was to provide him with a house. At Windy Hills a small house was built, and the garden laid out by the monks, some of whom shared the house.

Mary, Queen of Scots stayed for a couple of days at Kinloss Abbey and "Apples from the Chanter's garden" were on the menu card for the Queen.

The monks' steps, built into the garden wall, can still be seen, and with its magnificent herbaceous borders and grass walks, the monks' garden has still a wonderful atmosphere of peace and tranquillity.

Drum Castle Tower in Aberdeenshire was built about 1300 A.D.

Drum Castle, Aberdeenshire, the home of the Irvine family for over 600 years. The Tower has remained essentially the same, showing the early type of battlements. The original entrance would be at the level of the first floor by a moveable wooden stair, long since replaced by stone steps. The walls of the vaulted dungeon or store-room in the basement are twelve feet thick, pierced by two narrow loops at the east and west ends, with an inside stair within the thickness of the east wall up to the Common Hall on the first floor. There is a well in a recess in the basement and a stone basin with a drain to the outside close by.

From the first floor there is a spiral stone stair up to the Upper Hall which has a pointed barrel vault ceiling and is lighted by windows on every side. In the north-west corner there is a garde-robe with a foot-square drain running down twenty-five feet through the solid wall.

The house was added to the early tower in 1619 and is still occupied by the Irvine family, descendants of William de Irvine, Armour-bearer and Clerk-Register to King Robert the Bruce, to whom he gave the Lands and Forest of Drum, (previously a Royal Forest,) with the Tower of Drum, in 1323 A.D. The Royal Charter is still in the possession of the Irvine family. There is a 15th century Brew House adjoining the North wall of the Tower.

The house which was added to Drum Castle Tower in 1619 A.D.

The 16th century stair tower at Luffness House.

The small upper windows in the 16th century stair tower at Luffness still show the slots for moveable frames, on which parchment or transparent skins would be stretched before the use of glass in houses. The spiral stair was widened in the mid-18th century.

An early 16th century type of gunloop can be seen in the base of the tower and a small stair turret is corbelled, with the corbelling supported on a squinch—a small stone arch—as at Pilmuir only a few miles away.

Luffness House, East Lothian, the home of Major and Mrs. Hope, is of great architectural interest in that the house incorporates the remains of a great castle, probably 13th century, of which the extensive earthworks and moat can still be seen. This castle was partially demolished by the English in the Mid-16th century, after which the 16th century stair-tower and turrets were superimposed, with further additions in the early 17th century, and again in modern times.

The main block has immensely thick walls, with mural chambers, and was probably the keep of the early fortress. The bones of three Norse raiders still lie under the stone flooring of the vaulted chamber in the east gable, and the Vikings were finally driven off at the Battle of Largs in 1265.

On the corbelled S.W. angle-turret with its gun-loops is a panel dated 1584 with the initials of Sir Patrick Hepburn and his wife Isobel Haldane, who acquired Luffness at the Reformation.

Dunvegan Castle, Isle of Skye, the 13th century home of the Chief of the Clan MacLeod, where the family have lived for seven hundred years.

The Sea Gate, where the MacLeod galleys came alongside to discharge their passengers, the curtain wall and the well in the middle of the courtyard are all thought to date from the 13th century. About a hundred years later, towards the end of the 14th century, the great Tower of Dunvegan, with its pit or prison, was added at the North-East corner of the rock, probably by Malcolm, the 3rd Chief. The Fairy Tower was built at the S.E. corner early in the 16th century and buildings connecting the two towers were erected by Rory Mor in 1623.

The Sea Gate at Dunvegan Castle seen from within the walls.

Until 1748 the Sea Gate was the only entrance to Dunvegan but it was originally much wider, according to Dr Douglas Simpson, and was defended by a portcullis. The grooves for the portcullis can still be seen and the stonework beside the grooves has been worn away by the guards sharpening their blades on it.

It is said that King James V visited Dunvegan on his Hebridean voyages in 1536 and 1540, Boswell and Dr Johnson in 1773, and Sir Walter Scott in 1814.

The silver-mounted horn of Rory Mor at Dunvegan Castle, thought to date from the 14th century with 16th century silver work.

One of the MacLeod treasures at Dunvegan Castle is this huge ox horn banded with silver which tradition says was taken from a bull killed by the 3rd Chief in the 14th century. Mr Ian Finlay of the Royal Scottish Museum considers that this is possible, but that the Celtic silver work is of 16th century date done by a "Ceard" craftsman, or travelling tinker. In the National Museum of Antiquities of Scotland there is a brooch, (NG 231) with similar decoration.

Each Chief has to drain the horn empty of claret at a single draught, and John MacLeod of MacLeod did this at his recent coming of age celebrations. The horn holds nearly half a gallon.

Castle Leod. Ross and Cromarty, home of the Earl of Cromartie.

A much earlier building on this site was extensively altered by Sir Roderick Mackenzie, grandfather of the Ist Earl of Cromartie, and completed in 1615 with corbelling and other details of richness and variety.

The date of 1605 over the door commemorates Sir Roderick's marriage to Margaret MacLeod, heiress of the Lews.

In 1746, after the defeat of the Jacobite army at Culloden, the Cromartie estates were confiscated and the castle was taken by the Hanoverian Lord MacLeod, but in 1777 the son of the attainted 3rd Earl of Cromartie regained possession of the Cromartie estates from George III and the family has occupied the Castle ever since.

The dormer windows on the North side have the initials RMK and MMC for Sir Roderick Mackenzie and his wife Margaret MacLeod.

A carved stone panel representing Mars even has IB carved on the halberd, after an engraving of 1528.

The entrance to the pleasance with the date 1604 and the coat-of-arms of Sir David Lindsay, and his initials and those of his wife. The blue and white lobelia planted in the recesses to give the chequered effect can be seen.

Edzell Castle Gardens in Angus are in the care of the Ministry of Public Building and Works and are open to the public.

Edzell Castle is now a ruin but the garden or pleasance with its twelve foot high heraldic walls and Garden House built by Sir David Lindsay, Lord Edzell, in 1604, has survived.

Lord Edzell was a cultured man who had travelled widely on the Continent and the carved stone panels are copied from engravings by Meister IB of Nuremberg.

In summer blue and white lobelia is planted in the recesses of the wall to carry out the heraldic device of the blue and white fess-chequy of the coat-of-arms of the Lindsays.

View from within one of the round towers at Glenbervie.

An unusual view showing the immensely thick walls, the vaulted roof and the narrow slit window for defence, as seen from within. Glenbervie Castle was said to have been besieged and burned after the Battle of Brechin in 1452, rebuilt in the 15th and 16th centuries, added to in the 17th century and again in Victorian times, though I understand that the Victorian additions to the South tower have very recently been removed by the present owner.

Glenbervie House, Kincardineshire, a fortified house which incorporates a mediaeval castle.

Glenbervie House is on an ancient site for Glenbervie Castle was a stronghold of the Melville family from the 12th century, and was visited by Edward of England during the first English invasion of 1296. The nucleus of the present house is a mediaeval castle, probably dating from the 14th century, of which the two massive round towers could be the angle-towers of a courtyard type of castle. In both towers there are splayed gunloops and slit windows. The Douglas family were lairds of Glenbervie Castle for many years.

The south front of Fyvie Castle, Aberdeenshire, a royal castle until the late 14th century, now the property of the Fyvie Trustees.

Fyvie Castle was a royal residence from the time of King William the Lion (1165-1214) and was granted by King Robert II to his eldest son, later Robert III, but in the late 14th century the early castle was replaced by the building of the east tower by Sir Harry Preston. The west tower was built about a hundred feet away by the Meldrums in the 16th century, and at the end of the 16th century Fyvie passed to Lady Seton. Her son Alexander Seton, Baron Fyvie, and later Earl of Dunfermline and Chancellor of Scotland heightened the two existing towers and joined them together in the magnificent south front 150 feet long. The central arched gatehouse tower is known as the Seton tower.

In his book "The Scottish Castle" Stewart Cruden discusses the question of French influence and decides that "although the result is French the means are not. The squat corner roundels upon corbels, the stepped string courses and the surface blankness of the main residential blocks which link the towers are typically Scottish of the Aberdeenshire school of the late 16th and early 17th centuries."

Portrait of Colonel William Gordon of Fyvie painted by Pompeo Batoni in 1766. Height 102 ins., width 74 ins.

Pompeo Batoni, a pupil of Massucci, was working in Rome between about 1740-1770 and was the most fashionable and prolific portrait painter of his time. He also painted altar-pieces and allegories, and introduced the allusive portrait, with buildings or scenes of topographical interest in the background,—in this case the Colosseum at Rome.

Colonel Gorden of Fyvie was a professional soldier and is shown here in the uniform of the Queen's Own Royal Highlanders, the 105th Regiment of Foot.

The Yett of 1468 at the entrance to the wild garden at Guthrie Castle.

Yetts are a type of iron gate peculiar to Scotland in which the bars penetrate each other, and this is reversed in opposite quarters so that no bar can be pulled out. They were hung behind the wooden entrance door of the castle so that if the door were burned the defenders could shoot between the bars of the yett.

Guthrie Castle, Angus, built by Sir David Guthrie in 1468 and inhabited by the Guthries of Guthrie ever since. The castle and gardens are open to the public on certain afternoons.

It was in 1468 that King James III granted a warrant to build a castle and a yett to Sir David Guthrie, the King's Treasurer, although there was probably a stronghold before that date.

The castle built in 1468 is the high square tower which the Guthrie family occupied until about 1760 when they built a house close by and moved there. Then in 1848 John Guthrie of Guthrie connected the Tower to the house and added on the drawing-room.

The walled garden seen from the Great Hall of the tower. At Guthrie the garden slopes to the south facing the castle and the yew hedges are about eighty-five years old, but the garden is very much older although the actual date is not known.

In the Great Hall of the tower, which is almost unaltered, there are some fragments of 15th century murals from the Guthrie Aisle.

The wild garden at Guthrie Castle in May when it is open to the public.

Azaleas, maples, bulbs, meconopsis and primulas have been cleverly planted in a birch wood and the effect is quite enchanting.

The south front of Kellie Castle, Fife home of the sculptor Hew M. Lorimer.

The Oliphant family owned Kellie Castle from 1360 until 1613 when they sold it to Thomas Erskine, Viscount Fenton, who was created 1st Earl of Kellie the next year.

The castle is T-shaped and the north-west tower in the 15th century was probably a square tower with a courtyard enclosed by a curtain wall. In the 16th century the tower was heightened and new buildings were erected, using the curtain wall as the base. This may account for the initials MH and the datc 1573 being placed so high up on the east tower. The two towers, standing about fifty feet apart on the old curtain walls, were then joined together by the central block and the corbelling, turrets and dormer windows added in 1606 by the 5th Lord Oliphant.

The north front of Kellie Castle from the old walled garden.

The earliest tower is on the right and there are staircase towers which project, for owing to the various additions at different periods, Kellie Castle has five separate staircases.

The Vine Room at Kellie has an unusual coved ceiling with delicate plasterwork of 1676.

In the 19th century Kellie Castle was left empty for years but was fortunately rescued in 1878 by Professor Lorimer, father of the famous architect Sir Robert Lorimer, and the castle is now owned and occupied by his son Hew M. Lorimer, the well-known sculptor.

The old banqueting hall at Kellie Castle has a fine plasterwork ceiling dating from 1676, showing the arms of the Earls of Kellie. The hall is fifty feet long with windows on three sides.

Cawdor Castle, Nairn, the home of Earl and Countess Cawdor and the legendary scene of Macbeth, from across the river.

Cawdor Castle stands high above a tributary of the river Nairn on a rock foundation, and the high square keep, which is the oldest part, dates from about 1390. This early tower was enclosed by a very thick curtain wall with a parapet walk overlooking the dry moat of the outer defences—dry because of the height above the river.

In times of danger all the animals would be driven inside the curtain wall. The entrance to the castle was by ladder to the first floor, the ladder being pulled up afterwards. There was no staircase from the ground floor to help an enemy gain entrance; the stair led up from the Great Hall on the first floor to the upper floors of the tower.

This shows the 17th century additions when the curtain wall was used for the foundations.

The entrance to Cawdor Castle with parts of the original curtain wall on either side of the drawbridge over the dry moat.

On the battlements at Cawdor.

The corner turrets were a feature of early Scottish castles long before the period of French influence in Scotland. From about 1300 to the end of the 15th century they were open rounds for defence, in the 16th century they were roofed over as at Cawdor, and later became purely ornamental.

Cawdor Castle gardens as seen from the battlements. The gardens are usually opened to the public twice a year under Scotland's Gardens Scheme.

The dining-room at Cawdor is in the 17th century addition which was built on top of the early curtain wall, and overlooks the river far below. The mantelpiece commemorates the marriage in 1510 of Muriel, heiress of Cawdor, to John Campbell, 3rd son of the Earl of Argyll, from whom the present Earl Cawdor is descended.

The Blue Room at Cawdor dates from the period between 1660 and 1670 when Sir Hugh Campbell and his wife Lady Henrietta Stuart, sister of the Earl of Moray, were building on the early curtain wall and turning a fortified tower into a home. The date 1667 can be seen on the stone mantelpiece.

The room on the top floor of the early tower at Cawdor has a vaulted stone roof, stone window seats and a small recess high up in the wall, probably an early type of strong room for valuables, as this room would be defended to the last.

The Tapestry Bedroom at Cawdor where the walls are still hung with the tapestries specially imported from Arras in 1682. In the Charter Room are documents showing not only the price paid for each tapestry but the cost of each stage of their journey by ship to Leith, Dysart and right to the mouth of the local river Findhorn.
Even the bed-hangings are thought to be the original 17th century red velvet hangings mentioned in the Inventory of 1688.
In the foreground is a walnut day-bed of the time of Charles II.

Borthwick Castle, Midlothian, circa 1430, showing part of the curtain wall and gatehouse.

In 1430 Sir William of Borthwick was granted a licence by James I to build "a castle or fortalice, to surround it with walls and ditches, to defend it with gates of brass and iron."

Borthwick is one of the finest late mediaeval castles in Britain, dated, complete and unaltered, according to Stewart Cruden in his book "The Scottish Castle". It is built on the double L-plan, with walls 12-14 feet thick at the base. and standing 110 feet high, containing eight storeys in the north tower. Part of the curtain wall is shown, with its gatehouse which has had a portcullis and drawbridge.

During the Second World War this magnificent castle was put to good use for Scotland's most valuable art treasures and irreplaceable books and manuscripts were stored here within those massive walls, and guarded day and night.

A 15th century buffet recess in the Great Hall at Borthwick Castle.

The Great Hall in Borthwick is 50 feet long, with a pointed barrel vaulted ceiling, and the buffet recess is near the nine foot wide hooded fireplace at the south end. At the north end there has been a passage cut off by a screen, and there is a carved canopy with miniature ribbed vaulting over a handsome wash-basin with a drain to the outside.

Buffets were used for the display of silver or pewter, and the small heraldic shields above would be coloured and gilded. The walls and woodwork would also be painted and hung with rich tapestries so that the general effect would be one of colour and variety, very different from the bare walls of castles to-day.

Kilravock Castle, Nairn, where the Rose family have owned land since the late 13th century.

The square tower surmounted by a caphouse and barbican was built by Hugh Rose, the 7th Chief, and in 1553 Hugh Rose, 10th Baron of Kilravock, began to build a Manor House on to the old keep. He was a very influential man and kept the peace in the district.

The bedroom at Kilravock at the top of the early tower where Mary Queen of Scots slept in 1562. The walls here are seven feet thick as can be seen at the window, and through the archway is the spiral stone stair which leads up to the battlements.

In 1562 Mary Queen of Scots was his guest at Kilravock, and there is a letter from her to her "truist friend the Baron of Kilravock". She asks him as one of her "special friendis" to see that "good rule and order is kept within his bounds".

Looking into the walled garden at Airlie Castle with its clipped yew trees and grass walks.

The entrance to Airlie Castle, in Angus, home of the Earl and Countess of Airlie.

Sir Walter Ogilvy of Lintrathen, Lord High Treasurer and Master of the Household to James I was granted a licence by the King in 1431 to erect "his tower of Eroly" in the form of a castle. The site is at the junction of the rivers Isla and Melgum, with deep gorges on either side, leaving only one side to be defended. Here a wall 35 feet high and 10 feet thick was built behind a deep ditch 30 feet wide, over which would be a drawbridge with a portcullis at the gateway.

In 1641 Airlie Castle was looted and burned by Argyle, and little more than the massive wall survived, so the Ogilvy family moved to Cortachy Castle until the late 18th century.

The gate-tower has probably been altered in the 16th century, and the caphouse opens on to a parapet and a walk along the top of the wall.

Airlie Castle as rebuilt in 1792, behind the wall of 1432, by Lord Ogilvy after his return from thirty years' exile in France for his part in the Jacobite Rising of 1745.

A corner of the drawing-room at Airlie Castle.

A painting of Blanche, Countess of Airlie, by Clifford can be seen to the right of the mantelpiece, and the oval portrait is of Edith, Viscountess Sudley, the mother of Mabell, Countess of Airlie.

There are Viennese china dessert plates above pieces of Dresden china on the shelves, and from this window you look sheer down to the river 117 feet below.

Also in the drawing-room at Airlie Castle is this fine marquetry cabinet containing an interesting collection of white china, including the Lippizaner horses from Vienna. The portrait is of Juliette, Baronne d'Anspach, widow of Jean Paul Lejoyen, Comte de Grandpré, who married the Duc de Bourgogne in 1784.

The dining-room at Airlie is in the vaulted basement of the early castle which survived the destruction by Argyle in 1641.
Regimental china figures show up well on the Regency mahogany table with its reeded edge, and the mahogany chairs are Chinese Chippendale in design.
The portrait above the sideboard is of Cardinal Beaton.

Bedroom at Airlie Castle.

A portrait by Zucchero, height 3 ft. 6 ins., width 2 ft. 6 ins.
Federigo Zucchero came to Britain in the 16th century for a short period and there are several portraits of Mary, Queen of Scots, which are attributed to him.

Cortachy Castle, Angus, the home of Lord and Lady Ogilvy.

There is a tradition that there was a castle at Cortachy in the 13th century, and that King Robert the Bruce used it as one of his hunting lodges. Certainly there have been Ogilvys at Cortachy since 1473, although it belonged to another branch of the family until the Earl of Airlie bought it from Thomas Ogilvy of Inverquharity in 1625. After the burning of Airlie Castle in 1641. it became the principal seat of the Ogilvy family.

An eye-witness account of life in Scotland in the 15th century is given in a detailed secret report in cipher from a Spaniard reporting to his sovereigns, dated 25th July, 1498, which can be read in "Scottish Pageant" by the late Agnes Mure Mackenzie, the historian.

After describing King James IV, who spoke seven languages, the country and the people, Don Pedro continues: "The houses are good, all built of hewn stone and provided with excellent doors, glass windows, and a great number of chimneys. All the furniture that is used in Italy, Spain and France is to be found in their dwellings. It has not been bought in recent times only, but inherited from preceding ages." So life in the 15th century may not have been quite so bleak as we have been led to believe.

In the time of Mary, Queen of Scots the Scottish Customs duties show that imports included furs from Norway and the Baltic, fine leather from Spain and Russia, cloth of gold and silver, Chinese and Italian silks, carpets from Venice and Turkey, carved ivory, coral, jet and amber, velvet dressing cases with silver fittings, jewels, exotic foods and the wines of Cyprus, Spain, Italy and France.

The drawing-room at Cortachy Castle.

The door opens into a room in the early tower and above the door can be seen a very small musician's gallery, for the family piper perhaps, or a fiddler.

In 1650 Charles II stayed a night at Cortachy, for the Ogilvys were staunch Royalists, and as a result in the following year Cromwell's troops sacked the castle.

Lady Ogilvy's sitting-room at Cortachy Castle.

Lady Ogilvy's bedroom at Cortachy Castle.

Saddle cloth at Cortachy Castle.

Saddle cloth of velvet and cloth of silver used by Lady Ogilvy when she rode to Prince Charlie's Court at Holyrood in 1745.

Lord Ogilvy had raised the Angus Regiment for Prince Charlie, and his parents had sold their jewels and plate to equip them. In October 1745 the Angus Regiment were on guard duty at Holyrood Palace and the beautiful Lady Ogilvy joined her husband, and became a shining light at Prince Charlie's Court. After the Jacobites were defeated at Culloden—where Lady Ogilvy had held a spare horse for her husband—Lord Ogilvy escaped to France, but his wife was arrested and imprisoned in Edinburgh Castle, from whence she escaped with the help of her sister, and rejoined her husband in France.

Lord Ogilvy, known as "Le Bel Ecossais", was very popular in France, and was allowed to enlist exiled Scots in "Le Regiment Ogilvy", but it was only after 32 years of exile in France that he was allowed to return to Scotland and in 1792 he restored Airlie Castle.

Outside the curtain wall at Craigievar showing through the archway the only door to the castle. The curtain wall is 15 feet thick and there are recesses within the archway for the guards.

There is still only one door to Craigievar with its own iron yett, but this is at ground floor level, unlike the earlier castles which were built for defence.

The Great Hall at Craigievar.

In the Great Hall at Craigievar the barrel vaulted roof with groined centre is richly decorated with plasterwork, thought to be the work of the same plasterer who had been employed at Glamis in 1620.

The Royal Arms of Scotland over the fireplace resemble the well-known overmantel at Muchalls Castle dated 1624.

The Hall is lined with finely-carved oak wainscoting, with a 6 feet mediaeval screen and a very small musician's gallery at each end, perhaps a piper and a fiddler.

Craigievar Castle, now the property of the National Trust for Scotland, with the castle open to the public.

The Mortimer family had already begun to build a castle at Craigievar when they sold the estate in 1610 to William Forbes, brother of the Bishop of Aberdeen, who had "made a goodlie pile merchandizing at Dantzick."

William Forbes completed the castle in 1626, and although the exterior is still that of a fortified tower there are magnificent plaster ceilings in almost every room, and Renaissance cupolas and balustrades.

Craigievar has survived intact, the only alterations being the 18th century pine panelling in the bedrooms, and the replacement of the stone slates of the roof in 1826. A unique survival is the small circular tower and part of the 15 foot thick curtain wall which originally surrounded the castle.

Craigievar has remained in the possession of the Forbes family until it was bought by the National Trust for Scotland in 1963.

The housekeeper's box-bed at Craigievar is now a bathroom.

In the Queen's Room at Craigievar.

The portraits of Sir William Forbes, the 5th baronet, and his wife, who was a daughter of the 12th Lord Sempill, are by Sir Henry Raeburn. The receipts are framed alongside —sixteen guineas for the two portraits and six guineas for the frames.

Even in the bedrooms at Craigievar there are fine plasterwork ceilings.

Barra Castle, Aberdeenshire, a fortified laird's house.

In "The Fortified House in Scotland" Nigel Tranter mentions that the family of King lived at Barra for 300 years from the mid-13th century, so that there was probably an early nucleus on which to build. In 1598 the Barony of Barra was given by James VI to George Seton of Meldrum, who had bought Barra from James King. On the central chimney stack is the date 1614, with MGS for George and Mary Seton above one of the windows, with the Seton arms. The turrets were probably of the Seton period but the vaulted kitchen and cellar are thought to be 16th century.

Further additions were made about 1700 and 1755 forming three sides of a courtyard with a wall for the fourth.

Barra Castle from the terrace garden. There was a large walled garden in the olden days, with a garden house at one corner, and part of the garden house still stands.

China display shelves which were found behind the panelling at Barra.

The central block is the oldest part of Barra Castle, and the Hall on the first floor was originally a much larger room, now subdivided to make a dining-room and drawing-room. A small tower room opens off the drawing-room with a newel stair down to the cellar.

The Hall at Barra Castle, now the drawing-room.

The 16th century kitchen at Barra Castle, with its stepped window and barrel vaulted roof is in the basement of the earliest portion.

Panelling of about 1690, and an 18th century bed at Barra Castle.

Barra Castle, one of the most attractive of the smaller Scottish castles, was not spoiled in Victorian times by "improvements" in bringing the castle up to date. As a result this panelling of about 1690 has survived intact, still with its secret door behind the china plaque.

The elegant bed is of 18th century date, and the hand-embroidered coverlet of the period of William and Mary, late 17th century.

Balbithan House, Aberdeenshire.

The Chalmers family owned Balbithan from before 1490 for two hundred years, and lived formerly at Old Balbithan about a mile away. In order to have more privacy they moved to this site but the two wings of this L-shaped house appear to be of different dates, the south wing on the right being the older.

In his researches for "The Fortified House in Scotland" Nigel Tranter has found an entry in the Register of the Great Seal referring to the Newbigging of Balbithan in February 1600, and a charter of 1635 is given at the "novo loco de Balbithan"—the new place of Balbithan. The sundial on the west wing dated 1679 may be the date when the west wing was added to the existing south wing.

During the time of the Covenanters Montrose and his friends met at Balbithan, and after the battle of Culloden in 1746 Prince Charlie's soldiers were said to have been given shelter here. The tradition of hospitality is still maintained.

A room in the older wing where the walls are so thick that they contain a mural staircase from the wine cellar to the Hall above.

Inside the 15th century Lethington Tower.

The vaulted Great Hall is thirty-nine feet long with four deeply recessed windows, The walls are 8-10 feet thick, and in mediaeval times they would be hung with tapestries and decorated in colour.

Lennoxlove, or Lethington Tower, East Lothian, home of the Duke and Duchess of Hamilton, is open to the public in summer.

This was the home of William Maitland of Lethington, Secretary to Mary, Queen of Scots, and for centuries the Maitlands were prominent in Scottish history.

The massive tower is of the 15th century or earlier, built on the L-plan with the entrance in the re-entrant angle, while the battlements have rounded angle bartizans for defence, and projecting gargoyles to carry the rain water clear of the tower. A mansion was added to the old fortalice in the 17th century, with further alterations later.

Frances Stewart, daughter of Lord Blantyre, was educated in France, and at the Court of Louis XIV before being appointed a Maid of Honour at the Court of Charles II. She was a famous beauty and Charles was fascinated by "La Belle Stuart", but she repulsed him and eloped with the Duke of Richmond and Lennox. At her death, Lethington Tower was purchased by her Trustees for a Blantyre cousin, and renamed Lennoxlove in accordance with the terms of her will.

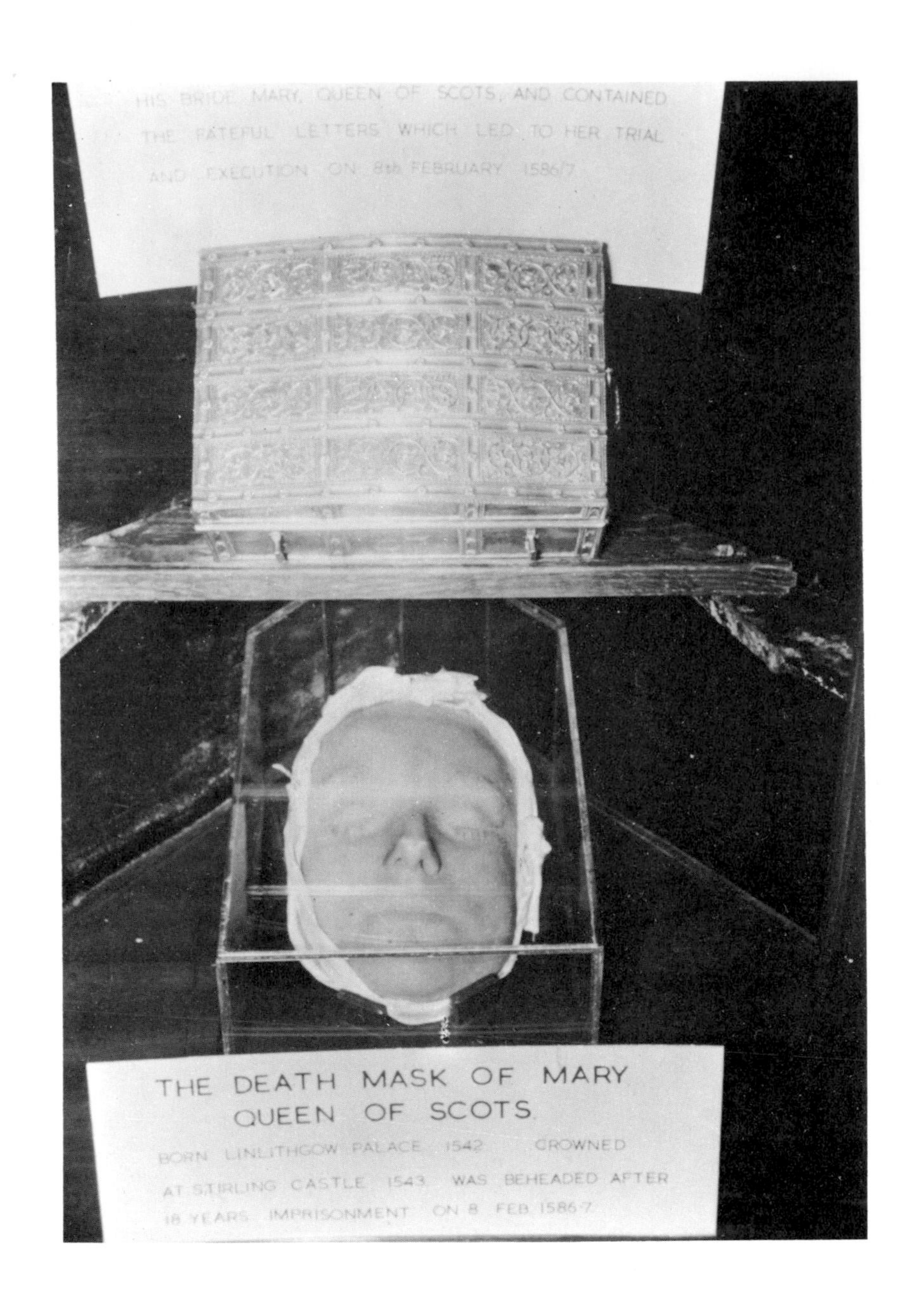

The death mask of Mary, Queen of Scots and the silver casket which contained letters which led to her execution by Elizabeth. There is considerable doubt as to whether the letters were or were not forgeries.

Cabinet and work-table given by Charles II to "La Belle Stuart".

The cabinet is of tortoiseshell inlaid with ivory and may be from the Louvre workshops of Andre-Charles Boulle, where he worked under the personal protection of Louis XIV.

The marquetry work table on the right is of ebony inlaid with pewter. On the wall behind the cabinet can be seen 17th century embroidered birds and flowers (see Traquair) appliqued to 18th century silk damask.

A magnificent silver toilet service with the monograms and coronet of "La Belle Stuart" as Duchess of Richmond and Lennox was found in the attic at Lennoxlove about 1900. It is of French workmanship of about 1680, and can now be seen in the Royal Scottish Museum in Edinburgh.

Craigston Castle, Aberdeenshire.

The Urquharts were hereditary Sheriffs of Cromarty from the time of David II (1329-71) and John Urquhart built this E-plan castle between 1604 and 1607.

The rectangular block with projecting wings joined by an arch is reminiscent of Fyvie Castle only a few miles away.

At Craigston there is elaborate corbelling as if for square angle turrets at each outer angle but apparently these were never built. Inside the castle there is excellent woodwork with a fine series of carved oak panels of the early 17th century.

The elaborately corbelled parapet at Craigston with carved figures representing jousting knights and a piper in the centre blowing his chanter.

The ivory Horn of Leys at Crathes Castle is said to have been given by King Robert the Bruce to Alexander de Burnard, or Burnett, with the charter of the lands of Leys in 1323, the horn being the symbol of land tenure. The Horn of Leys is still the property of the Burnett family but must never leave the castle.

Crathes Castle, Aberdeenshire, now owned by the National Trust for Scotland and open to the public.

Crathes Castle has been continuously occupied by the same family, the Burnetts of Leys, ever since they built the castle between 1553 and 1596, until they handed it over to the National Trust for Scotland with an endowment for its upkeep in 1951.

Crathes is a magnificent example of Scottish baronial architecture of the Aberdeenshire school. It is built on the L-plan, with plain wall surfaces below, blossoming out above with ornate corbelling, round and square turrets and dormer windows with quaint finials.

On the south front of the castle can be seen a group of three coats-of-arms, the centre one being the Royal Arms of Scotland showing that the Burnett laird was a tenant in chief holding his land directly from the king.

The view from an upper room of the castle. The gardens at Crathes Castle date from 1702 when the yew hedges were planted, and both the castle and the gardens are well worth visiting.

One of the fine painted ceilings at Crathes Castle. This one is in the Chamber of the Nine Muses, where in addition to the Muses, there are figures of Virtues, Wisdom, Justice, Faith, Hope and Charity, with the arms of Alexander Burnett and his wife and the date 1599.

Oak bed at Crathes Castle.

An oak four-poster bed made for Alexander Burnett and his wife Katherine Gordon in 1594. This is one of several of the original pieces of furniture made in the 16th century for the Burnett family, with their armorial bearings, carved portraits, and the date 1594. The bedspread and hangings are of Jacobean embroidery.

Delgatie Castle, Aberdeenshire, an ancient stronghold of the Clan Hay, Earls of Erroll, is the home of Captain Hay of Hayfield, and is open to the public on certain afternoons in summer.

For their part in the War of Liberation King Robert the Bruce made the Chief of the Hays Hereditary Lord High Constable of Scotland, combining the duties of Commander-in-Chief and Earl Marshal.

At the Battle of Flodden in 1513 the Chief of the Clan Hay, with Lord Hay of Yester, Sir Gilbert of Delgatie, and eighty-seven other Chieftains and officers of the name of Hay were killed beside their King, together with the whole of their following, between the ages of sixteen and sixty.

The high square keep of five storeys and a garret probably dates from the 16th century, although earlier work may be included. In the 17th century a tall gabled house was added, blocking the original entrance, with subsequent additions at a lower level.

In the original entrance lobby there is a ribbed and groin-vaulted ceiling, as there is also in the Hall on the first floor, where the ribs spring from corbels in the angles, the apex being ornamented with a boss bearing the arms of the Hays of Errol.

An open-timber painted ceiling at Delgatie Castle dated 1597.

At the top of the early tower is this unusual painted ceiling with strange animals, sphinxes and fishes between the beams, and a monogram of Andrew Hay of Delgaty and his wife Barbara Forbes. Along the beams are painted texts from a "Treatis of Morall philosophye containing the sayings of the wyse", published in 1567.

Painted ceilings were fashionable in Scotland from about 1550 for nearly a hundred years and are thought to be the work of local craftsmen influenced by designs from the Continent, particularly Scandinavia.

In his book "Painting in Scotland from the 14th-17th centuries" Dr M. R. Apted says "In the 16th century there were many Scots who as courtiers, diplomats, soldiers, churchmen or merchants were familiar with foreign countries, and even more who were acquainted with their culture through the work of visiting craftsmen or from imported works of art."

The painted ceiling at Delgatie shows the texts on the beams. The blue and white Dutch tiles in the fireplace recess were used in many castles and houses in the east of Scotland in the 17th and 18th centuries. Leyden was one of the favourite universities for Scottish students, for a Scottish gentleman expected to study on the continent after completing his studies at one of the Scottish universities, of which Scotland had four before 1600 while England still only had Oxford and Cambridge in 1707.

This picture of the Virgin was discovered beneath the fioor of the Chapel and is thought to be by Morales, a pupil of Murillo, who painted in Madrid about 1650.

A walled garden in Fife which is mentioned in a document dated 1591.

This garden adjoins a house very like Ardullie and is a typical Scottish walled garden, having a mixture of flowers, fruit and vegetables.

In his book "The Scots Gard'ner", published in 1683, John Reid, head gardener to Sir George Mackenzie of Rosehaugh in Ross-shire, gives detailed instructions for laying out a garden, planting, grafting and budding. He recommends growing apples, pears, cherries, plums, gooseberries, raspberries and currants, and "for walls are apricocks (sic), peaches, nectarines, vines, figs, almonds, plums, etc" while melons he grew on a hot-bed. Strawberries he considers "a very fine and delicate fruit" and tells how to increase them from runners. Advice on growing artichokes, broad beans, kidney beans, peas, asparagus, lettuce, endive, spinach, parsley, garlic, shallots and onions, leeks, cole-flower (sic), cabbages, carrots, parsnips, beet-rave (beetroot) and a great many herbs and flowers is given in this fascinating book, reprinted in 1907.

Walled gardens have persisted in Scotland through the centuries, and the earlier gardens actually adjoined the house or were close by as we see at Milton Brodie, Cawdor Castle, Guthrie Castle, Kellie Castle, Drumkilbo, Barra Castle, Lennoxlove, Crathes Castle, Edzell Castle, Ardullie Lodge, Muchalls Castle, Ravelston, Pilmuir, Innes House and the Castle of Mey. This is also borne out at Inveresk, Midlothian, where there are a number of late 17th and 18th century houses all with walled gardens adjoining. It was the later gardens that were built at a distance from the house.

Ardullie Lodge, Ross-shire, a seventeenth century laird's house.

Ardullie Lodge is the home of Captain Patrick Munro of Foulis, Chief of the Clan Munro, and was formerly the Dower House on the Foulis estate. It is a typical laird's house of the late seventeenth century, with its harled finish, steeply pitched roof and crowstepped gables, a Continental influence much in evidence on the East coast of Scotland.

The panelled dining-room at Ardullie Lodge, a perfect setting for the Munro heraldic plates. Compare the fielded panels with the panelling in the Blue Room at Cawdor, where the mantelpiece is dated 1667.

A heraldic plate of the mid-eighteenth century.

From about 1725-1755 armorial china with the coats-of-arms of the great families of Scotland and England was imported from China and was ordered from merchants in Canton or through the East India Company.

The decoration was painted by hand from bookplates, engravings or sketches sent out to them. After 1755 some English armorial services were made at Worcester during the Dr Wall period, and later at Bristol, and many factories would make replacements of broken Chinese examples.

The Munro heraldic plates show the coat-of-arms of Munro of Foulis with the Chinese idea of Foulis Castle in the centre. This has no resemblance to the present castle, built in the second half of the 18th century, but may well represent the tower house or keep of an earlier castle.

Having been told that the castle overlooked the sea the Chinese artist has shown junks and sampans in the side panels, a charming touch which to my mind proves that those plates really were painted in China for the Munros of Foulis.

Muchalls Castle, Kincardineshire, built by the Burnetts of Leys between 1619 and 1627, is open to the public on certain days.

Muchalls was built by the Burnetts of Leys after they had completed Crathes Castle, in the new style of building, more domestic in character but still with a courtyard and defensive wall. An earlier fortress may be the foundation of the present building as the basement has vaulted roofs and very thick walls.

The gateway to the courtyard is flanked by triple shot-holes and the wall would originally be higher and surmounted by a parapet walk.

On the panel above the gateway is carved the inscription:— "This work begun on the east and north be Ar. Burnet of Leyis 1619. Ended be Sir Thomas Burnet of Leyis his sonne 1627".

The Great Hall at Muchalls showing the Royal Arms of Scotland dated 1624 above the fireplace.

This is only one of several fine plaster ceilings at Muchalls which include the heraldic designs of the Burnetts and their friends, with heads of Biblical characters.

Above the huge lintel stone are the Royal Arms of Scotland, painted and gilt, as borne in Scotland after the Union of the Crowns in 1603, (when James VI of Scotland succeeded to the English throne as James I of England), flanked by caryatides in the Renaissance manner.

The House of Monymusk in Aberdeenshire.

Monymusk is the home of Sir Francis Grant, Bt., and has been occupied by the Grant family since 1713 when they bought Monymusk estate from the Forbes family, who had owned it since the Reformation in 1560.

The round tower, with four storeys and vaulted basement, was probably one of the angle towers of the barmekin wall of the early castle, according to Dr. W. Douglas Simpson, but through the centuries Monymusk has been much altered.

The Priory of Monymusk in the 12th century was the home of the ancient Celtic church of the Culdees, but early in the 13th century was taken over by the Augustinians, and by the time of the Reformation the Priory buildings were in a ruinous condition.

The famous Monymusk Reliquary, mentioned in the 7th century, remained at Monymusk for 618 years before being bought for the nation in 1923. It can be seen at the National Museum of Antiquities in Edinburgh.

For centuries it was the duty of the Custodian to carry the Reliquary into battle at the head of the Scottish army. This was done before the Battle of Bannockburn in 1314, and the next year Bernard de Linton, Abbot of Arbroath, granted custody of the Reliquary to Malcolm of Monymusk.

Bernard de Linton was probably the author of the famous Declaration of Arbroath in 1320 which states "for so long as a hundred of us are left alive, we will yield in no least way to English dominion. We fight not for glory nor wealth nor for honours: but only and alone we fight for *freedom*, which no good man surrenders but with his life."

The Monymusk Madonna, height 3 ft. 7 ins., of carved and gilded wood, probably 16th century.

A certain air of mystery surrounds this beautiful statue, which, according to tradition has always been in the House of Monymusk along with the famous Monymusk Reliquary, since the days of the Priory of Monymusk in the 16th century.

Authorities consulted, including the Right Rev. Monsignor McRoberts, agree that this is a 16th century pre-Reformation piece, possibly of Flemish workmanship. Originally it would be designed to have a wire halo adorned with twelve stars.

The Great Hall at Monymusk.

Painted on stone at the end of the Great Hall of Monymusk are the Royal Arms of Scotland in the time of King James VI of Scotland before he became James I of England. The Forbes coat-of-arms is seen on the far right.

Dr W. Douglas Simpson considers that the Great Hall was in existence before the Reformation in 1560, and the Royal Arms fresco may date from the late 16th or early 17th century.

On the left of the fireplace is an aumbry, an early form of cupboard, and the corbelling on the right concealed a stair to the room above, while there was another stair below a trap door leading down to a well in the vaulted basement.

Portrait of Lady Grant by Allan Ramsay 1751, height 49 ins., width 39 ins.

Lady Grant was the third wife of Sir Archibald Grant Bt. of Monymusk, the famous agricultural reformer who introduced turnips as a field crop for winter feed, and also planted several million trees on his estate. He used to send his tenants packets of turnip seed for Christmas, and under his direction the land was drained and dykes built with the stones removed from the fields.

Before his time the system of infield and outfield farming was still in use but Sir Archibald Grant was growing clover at Monymusk, and stressings its importance, as early as 1720, and by mid-18th century a large variety of crops were being grown:—oats, barley, rye, wheat, pease, clover, rye grass, cabbage, turnips, potatoes and lint.

Sir Archibald Grant was married four times, outliving three of his wives. He was a tremendously hard worker, and wrote in his Journal about his second wife Anne Potts, "My wife is a dreadful Slug-a-bed, 'tis oft six of a morning ere she rises." This portrait however is not of the Slug-a-bed Lady Grant.

A 17th century curtain at Monymusk, wool embroidered on satin, partly re-backed.

The embroidered curtains in the drawing-room at Monymusk were originally hangings for four-poster beds, and were embroidered by the ladies of the Grant family. They were all good needlewomen but the best known of all was Anne Grant, sister of the agricultural reformer, who worked the huge petit point panel.

A petit point panel size 8 ft. 6 ins. by 6 ft. 6 ins. in the House of Monymusk, signed by Anne Grant, daughter of Sir Francis Grant, Lord Cullen, and dated 1750. The work-box which she used is shown open in front of the panel.

The dovecote at Pilmuir stands near the house inside the garden walls.

Bee-boles in the garden wall at Pilmuir ensured a supply of honey.

The north front of Pilmuir, East Lothian, a laird's house of the early 17th century.

Over the doorway of this attractive house is an heraldic panel with the arms and initials of William Cairns and his wife who built the house in 1624.

The house is T-shaped, with the entrance in the central stair tower, and the turret for the upper stair is corbelled out over a squinch, (a small stone arch set at an angle) also seen at Luffness House, a few miles away.

At one time Pilmuir must have been a large property for lairds were not allowed to keep more pigeons than could feed off their own land, and there is a very large dovecote inside the walled garden near the house.

A new entrance with steps up to the first floor has been made on the south front, and this is almost the only alteration since Pilmuir was built in 1624, but this is a house that is still a home, and gives the impression of having always been appreciated by its owners.

This aumbry, an early type of cupboard, was found behind the pine panelling in the drawing-room at Pilmuir, showing that the panelling is of later date, the fielded panels being similar to those at Ardullie and the Blue Room, Cawdor.
The Queen Anne walnut knee-hole writing-table in the window recess shows the thickness of the outer walls.

A corner of one of the bedrooms at Pilmuir showing an early type of window before the introduction of weights, a window seat and panelling.
On the top of the 18th century mahogany chest of drawers is a mahogany tea caddy and a miniature mahogany chest of drawers. The miniature chest is probably a test piece made by an apprentice cabinet-maker at the end of his years of apprenticeship.

The doorway at Dunderave with the date 1596, the initials of the builder and his wife, and "Behald the end: be nocht vyser nor the Hiestes", followed by the family motto, "I hoip in God" carved on the lintel stone.

Dunderave Castle, Argyllshire, a Clan Macnaughton castle, built in 1596, and restored about 1912 by Sir Robert Lorimer.

Cullen House, home of the Countess of Seafield, in Banffshire, which is open to the public on certain afternoons in summer.

Although a building on this site is mentioned in 1254 (Scottish Castles of the 16th & 17th century by O. Hill) the oldest part of the present building probably dates from 1543 when the 13th century Chapel of the Blessed Mary was elevated to the dignity of a Collegiate Church, and the six Prebends each had his "apartment and garden adjacent to the Church".

The Ogilvy family moved to Cullen from Findlater Castle about 1600 and Walter Ogilvy made extensive alterations and additions. In 1711 and again in 1858 there were further additions. In the grounds there is a single-arched stone bridge designed by Robert Adam.

Cullen is believed to have been the home of Martha, Countess of Carrick, the mother of King Robert the Bruce, and his first wife Elizabeth de Burgh died in Cullen, her heart being buried in Cullen Church. The king bequeathed £5 Scots per annum to the Priest of Cullen so that Masses could be said for her soul. A small sum is still paid to the Parish Minister of this now Protestant Church from the Common Good Fund administered by Cullen Town Council. This is presumably either the continuance of the Bruce Endowment, or a supplement which was apparently made by the Bailies and Community of Cullen at one time.

Portrait of James, 6th Earl of Findlater and 3rd Earl of Seafield (1714-1750), painted in Rome about 1740 by Agostino Massucci, at Cullen. Height 50 ins. width, 40 ins.

Agostino Massucci was Principal from 1736-38 of the Academy of St. Luke in Rome. He was a pupil of Carlo Maratta, and the master of Pompeo Batoni and Gavin Hamilton. Massucci was the most popular portrait painter in Rome at this time.

Portrait of James, 4th Earl of Findlater and 1st Earl of Seafield (1663-1730) by Sir Godfrey Kneller. Height 50 ins., width 40 ins.

He was Lord Chancellor of Scotland at the time of the Union of the Parliaments in 1707, and when he prorogued the Scottish Parliament for the last time he said: "There's an end of an auld sang".

A spirited rendering of the Royal Arms of Scotland at Cullen House shows that the painted coved ceiling probably dates from a year or two before the Union of the Crowns in 1603. There are also cloud forms and classical scenes, including the Siege of Troy.

Detail of the Siege of Troy on the painted ceiling at Cullen.

Portrait of Lady Margaret Ogilvy, daughter of James, 5th Earl of Findlater and 2nd Earl of Seafield, and second wife of Sir Ludovic Grant of Grant, height 50 ins., width 40 ins. signed and dated "A Ramsay 1744". This marriage is one of the most important links between the families of Ogilvy and Grant. The family name is now Ogilvy-Grant.

Portrait of Lady Sophia Hope, wife of the Earl of Findlater and 2nd Earl of Seafield, height 50 ins., width 40 ins., signed and dated "A Ramsay 1739". She is said to have sacrificed her "pin money" to help pay for the single-arched stone bridge over the Cullen Burn which was designed by Robert Adam, who also designed the entrance gate to the house.

In the Ogilvy bedroom at Cullen is this imposing bed, 7 ft. long by 5 ft. 11 ins. wide by 10 ft. high. The pelmets and curtains are all entirely hand-embroidered by Anne Smith and her friends in wool on fine linen. Anne Smith was the second wife of Brigadier Grant and had been a Maid of Honour to Queen Anne.

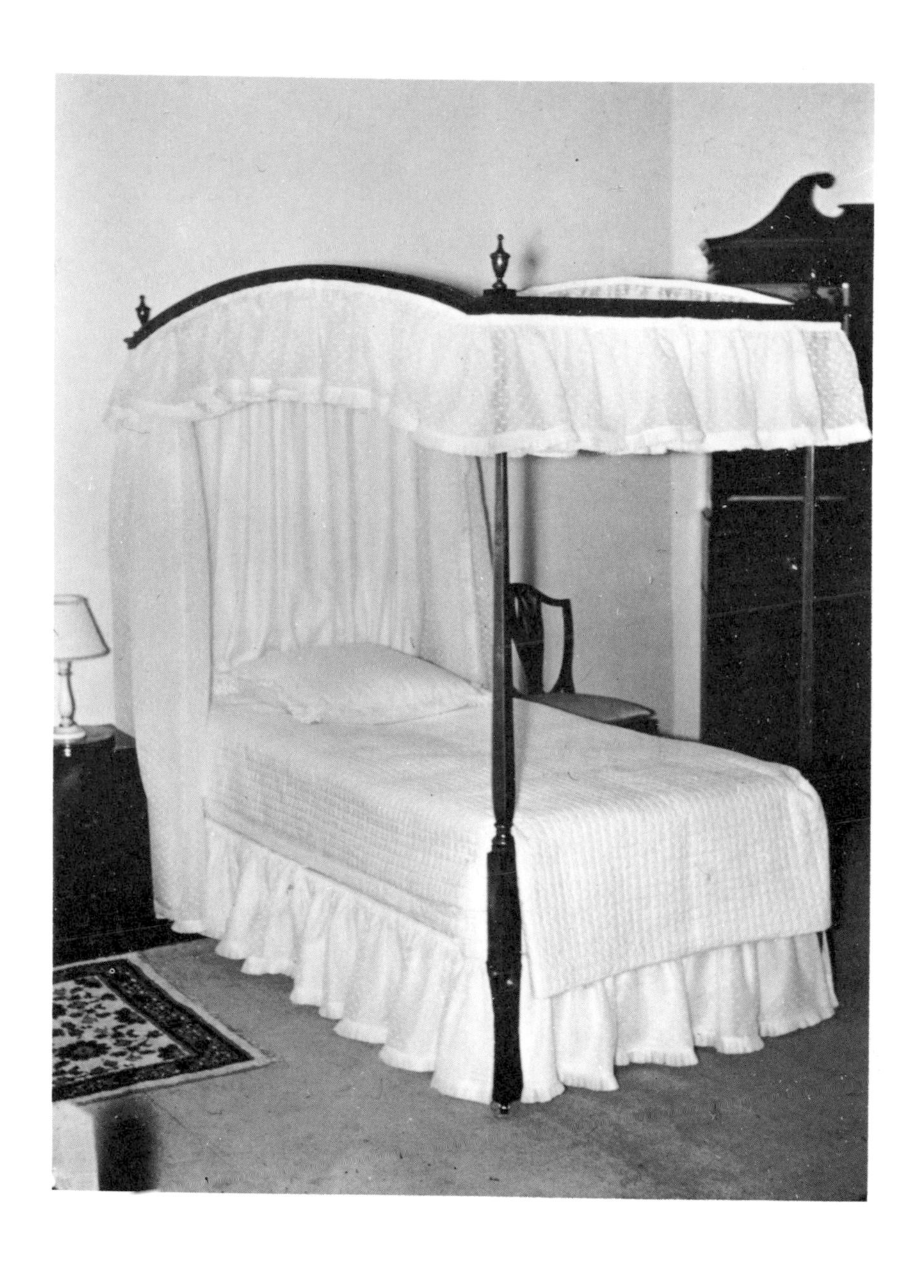

In the Dressing-room next door at Cullen is this graceful Hepplewhite bed, 6 ft. 9 ins. long, by 3 ft. 3 ins. wide, by 6 ft. 6 ins. high, draped in modern white spotted muslin.

Brodick Castle, Isle of Arran, now owned by the National Trust for Scotland. The castle and gardens are open to the public.

An early fortress, where King Robert the Bruce is said to have awaited his followers in 1306, the main structure dates from about 1500, was extended by Cromwell's troops in 1652, and was again added to in 1843-4 by the Marquess of Douglas and Clydesdale, son of the 10th Duke of Hamilton, when he married Princess Marie of Baden.

Primulas by the pool in Brodick Castle Gardens.

The beautiful gardens at Brodick Castle were created by the late Duchess of Montrose, granddaughter of Princess Marie of Baden.

Rhododendrons, azaleas, and a wide variety of flowers and shrubs grow happily in the soft climate of the Isle of Arran.

Drumkilbo House, Perthshire the home of Lord Elphinstone.

Drumkilbo House is near Meigle or Midgill, one of the oldest villages in Scotland. Meigle has a superb collection of Pictish sculptured stones, including one known as the Guinevere Stone, for tradition says that Arthur's Queen Guinevere is buried here.

King Robert the Bruce gave the lands of Drumkilbo to Morice de Tiry, and the Tyries owned Drumkilbo until the mid-17th century, when they sold the property to the Nairnes.

During the Commonwealth when Cromwell's General Monk was trying to subdue mid-Scotland, Lord Ogilvy (afterwards 2nd Earl) had his headquarters at Drumkilbo and led the Royalists most successfully against Cromwell's forces.

Portrait of Mary, Queen of Scots as a child, 12 ins. by $9\frac{3}{4}$ ins., 16th century, in the possession of Lord Elphinstone.

This charming portrait of Mary, Queen of Scots as a small girl was brought back from Spain about 100 years ago by one of Lord Elphinstone's ancestors. The artist is unknown, but the portrait is thought to be Spanish, painted in the 16th century.

One of a pair of Louis XVI tables at Drumkilbo from the Palace of Fontainbleau, width 3 ft. 2 ins., depth 1 ft. 9½ ins., height 2 ft. 5 ins.

This interesting writing table is one of a pair, both of which are marked with the French Royal Furniture Stamp and the Inventory number of the Palace of Fontainebleau.

Such authentic pieces are invaluable for dating French furniture.

The drawing-room at Drumkilbo House.

The thick walls of the 16th century Drumkilbo are the central portion of the present house, which was extended in 1920 to the design of the late Sir Robert Lorimer.

In 1963 Lord Elphinstone commissioned the late Robert Hurd, who did so much for Scottish architecture, to heighten a 19th century wing.

Sheltered by fine old trees from a busy main road, and surrounded by cleverly laid out gardens, Drumkilbo has a delightful atmosphere of peace.

This set of embroidered bed furnishings, consisting of tester, valance, bedhead, bedspread and cushion were all worked by Nina Cecilia, wife of the 14th Earl of Strathmore and Kinghorne, mother of Her Majesty, Queen Elizabeth, the Queen Mother, and grandmother of Lord Elphinstone. The cushion is embroidered with her cipher C.S. in coloured silks on fawn satin.

Four-poster bed at Drumkilbo.

Small sitting-room at Drumkilbo.

The mantelpiece in the small sitting-room was brought from Carberry Tower, near Edinburgh, the home of Lord Elphinstone's parents, the late Lord and Lady Elphinstone.

A collection of miniatures can be seen at each side of the mantelpiece, and the 18th century gilt mirror shows a reflection of some of the fine old trees surrounding Drumkilbo.

The pictures in this room are all Nasmyths.

Magnolia denudata in the garden at Drumkilbo, Perthshire.

Fullarton, an old farmhouse garden near Meigle, Perthshire.

The Tyries of Drumkilbo received their lands from King Robert the Bruce, and at about the same time the King bestowed a charter of certain lands in Meigle on his hereditary Fowler Galfredus Foullertoun on condition that he and his heirs should serve the Royal household with wildfowl while the King was in residence at the Castle of Forfar. The Fowler was to have entertainment with a boy, a servant and two horses.

Forfar and Glamis were ancient Royal demesnes, and in 1263, in the reign of Alexander III the Household accounts record payments for a stay of 29 weeks and include a payment for $4\frac{1}{2}$ chalders of corn for the wild boars (porci silvestris). Were wild boar reared for sport in 1263?

There is also payment for a gardener at the King's castle of Forfar in 1263, but we do not find purchases of vegetables, which were probably grown in the garden. In "Scotland in the Middle Ages" by Cosmo Innes, p 125 "We find the hortus olerum (or vegetable garden) an appendage of our better dwellings from the earliest records, and some kinds of kail have been used in Scotland by all classes as far back as we have any knowledge of".

Fullarton Castle, the home of the Foullertouns, long since demolished, stood near the present farmhouse and garden, a garden I have known all my life, for it belonged to a cousin of my father's and owes its beauty to his great interest in his garden.

The main entrance to Glamis Castle in the stairway tower, showing the many coats-of-arms.

Glamis Castle, Angus, for centuries a royal castle, and the childhood home of Her Majesty, Queen Elizabeth the Queen Mother, is open to the public on certain afternoons.

Glamis was a royal hunting lodge from the very earliest times and King Malcolm II is said to have died here in 1034. In the 14th century Glamis was given by King Robert II to Sir John Lyon, Chancellor of Scotland, who married his daughter, and it is still in the possession of their descendants.

In his book "The Fortified House in Scotland" Nigel Tranter is of the opinion that there was a tower in the 15th century, which was heightened in the 16th century, and added to and extended in the 17th century. The pre-15th century remains are probably incorporated in the lower portions of the 15th century tower, and the two massive round towers are all that remain of the flanking towers of a great courtyard connected to the central keep. The high central keep was remodelled by the 1st Earl of Kinghorne who was the laird of Glamis from 1578 to 1615.

The Great Hall at Glamis with the decoration of 1620.

The sitting-room in the royal apartments at Glamis. The thickness of the outer walls is shown by the large desk in the window recess.

Four-poster bed at Glamis Castle with bedhead and canopy embroidered by the late Countess of Strathmore and Kinghorne, mother of Her Majesty, Queen Elizabeth the Queen Mother.

The embroidery on the canopy shows the cipher SK beneath a coronet and the names of all her children, and the name Elizabeth in the circle just to the right of the bedpost represents Her Majesty, Queen Elizabeth the Queen Mother. On the bedhead there is an interesting design of thistles.

Innes House, Elgin, from the garden.

Innes House, the home of Captain Iain Tennant, was designed in 1640 for Sir Robert Innes of Innes by William Aytoun, the Master Mason who completed Heriot's Hospital in Edinburgh after the death of William Wallace.

The house is of the traditional L-plan with a square tower in the re-entrant angle, but with Renaissance detail in the design of the windows and their pediments. The building was not completed until 1653 and from the careful accounts kept by the laird we know that it cost £1,221:3:4 to build.

In 1912 a courtyard, surrounded by three wings, was added to the North of the house.

The dining-room at Innes House with a picture above the mantelpiece showing the house in the 18th century.

The Drawing-room at Innes House.

The original entrance to the Castle of Mey by the courtyard on the sea side was the only entrance in the early days, apart from a secret escape tunnel to the sea. Notice the gunloops at each side of the door.

In the late 18th century the 12th Earl of Caithness made a new entrance on the south front with steps leading up to it, but in the 19th century an enclosed double staircase was built out behind the present front door, and a dining-room wing added on to the west.

The Castle of Mey, Caithness, the northern home of Her Majesty, Queen Elizabeth the Queen Mother.

In 1556 George Sinclair, 4th Earl of Caithness, acquired the lands and Barony of Mey from Robert Stewart, Bishop of Caithness. The Bishop had already built a fortified store-house at Barrogill which the Earl now used as the nucleus of his castle, and the gunloops can still be seen on two levels.

On the right is a Caithness flagstone fence, made by standing flagstones on end, and beyond the castle wall can be seen the Orkney islands.

The 16th century castle from the eastern garden.

The castle was built on the traditional Z-plan with a tall battlemented tower with turrets whose conical roofs were removed by the 12th Earl and replaced by sham battlements.

A Queen's personal Coat-of-Arms in Edinburgh Tapestry 9 feet x 7 feet, which is in the dining-room of the Castle of Mey.

In 1950 the tapestry was woven to Her Majesty's order at the Dovecote Studios of the Edinburgh Tapestry Company, and shows her personal coat-of-arms with a decorative border incorporating flowers from her garden. It hangs on the end wall of the dining-room above the sideboard.

The design is by the late Sir Stephen Gooden and the artist-weavers were Ronald Cruikshank, John Louttit and Richard Gordon. Their initials can be seen by the right-hand border near the small beehive dovecote.

In the garden of the Dovecote Studios is a fine beehive dovecote of the late 16th century, all that remains of the castle of the Forresters of Corstorphine which stood close by, so the trade-mark of the Edinburgh Tapestry Company is a beehive dovecote.

Although it was not in the approved design the artist-weavers made sure that there was one four-leaved clover for luck.

The sunny dining-room in the Castle of Mey looks out over the old walled garden, with its traditional mixture of flowers, fruit and vegetables.

Through the window at the top of the double staircase can be seen the ER monogram with the thistle and the rose, carved by Hew Lorimer, the well-known Scottish sculptor.

A 17th century tapestry in the drawing-room at the Castle of Mey.

The drawing-room at the Castle of Mey is a lovely, sunny room with windows to the south and another window to the north looking over the sea to the Orkney Islands. One wall is covered by a huge 17th century tapestry of which the detail can be seen on the opposite page.

The Castle of Mey from the walled garden. This garden is mentioned by William Lithgow in 1628, and again by the Bishop of Caithness in 1762 who saw "plenty of apples, strawberries and some cherries", for the gardens have always been a feature of the castle at Barrogill.

View from the rock garden at Inverewe, Wester Ross.

This world-famous Highland garden, now under the National Trust for Scotland, was visited by nearly 100,000 people in 1966. Here plants from Australia, New Zealand, Chile and South Africa are flourishing, including Tree Ferns (Dicksonia antartica), many varieties of eucalyptus—some over 90 feet high—and the giant Forget-me-not (Myosotidium nobile).

It was in 1862 that the young Osgood Mackenzie, one of the Mackenzies of Gairloch, became the laird of the estates of Inverewe and Kernsary, which adjoined Gairloch. On the landward end of a rocky peninsula he built a house, planting pine trees beyond for shelter from the south-westerly gales. The coast of Wester Ross is warmed by the Gulf Stream, and by planting a variety of trees he found that with shelter from the winds he could grow almost anything. In fact a great many trees and shrubs which have to be grown under glass at Kew Gardens, London have been growing and flowering happily in the open at Inverewe for many years.

Northfield House, East Lothian, the home of W. Schomberg Scott, A.R.I.B.A., from the south.

Northfield House is built on the tradition L-plan with the original entrance in the re-entrant angle to the north leading to a turnpike stair. This view shows the oldest part of the house, dating from about 1580-90, which Joseph Marjoribanks, an Edinburgh burgess, bought in 1607. He added a wing at right angles facing west, and made a new main entrance in the south front and a wide scale and platt stair rising to the first floor.

Over the doorway is a moulded architrave inscribed "EXEP THE LORD BULD INWAE BULDS MAN", and a heraldic panel bearing the arms of Marjoribanks and Sympson, with the initials of his wife and himself, dated 1611.

At Northfield there are no gun loops and the house stands in a large walled garden. There are several very fine tempera painted ceilings, some of which have been uncovered by the present architect owner.

The walled garden at Ravelston House, with its Cedar of Lebanon and grass walks, was probably made in the 17th century.

In 1620 George Foulis, Master of His Majesty's Mint, purchased the lands of Ravelston, and in 1622 began to build a mansion which was completed in 1624, and the garden probably dates from about this time. In the early 19th century the house was almost totally destroyed by fire and the present mansion was built.

When Baroness, Lady Nairne, the well-known song writer, lived in Edinburgh she was very friendly with the Keiths, who then lived in Ravelston House, and used to sing at parties there in the early 19th century.

This photograph was taken in 1958, before the death of Lady Stewart-Clark, and is included in memory of a beautiful garden, now a scene of desolation in the hands of developers. Surely the City of Edinburgh might have kept up this fine old walled garden, which is within the city boundaries, and would have given pleasure to thousands.

List of Subscribers

Aberdeen County Library
Aberdeen University Library
Mrs. Edith Achilles, New York, U.S.A.
The Rt. Hon. the Earl of Airlie, K.T., Airlie Castle
Ancient Monuments Society
Royal Commission on the Ancient and Historical Monuments of Scotland
Messrs. Anderson & Sutherland
G. B. Anderson, Edinburgh
Angus & Kincardineshire County Library
Arbroath Public Library
His Grace The Duke of Argyll, Inveraray Castle
Messrs. James Askew & Són, Ltd., Preston
Atlanta Art Association, Georgia, U.S.A.
Mr. L. A. Bailey, Edinburgh
Bailey & Swinfen Exports Limited, London
Banff County Library
Banff School of Fine Arts, Alberta, Canada
Dr. W. D. Baston, Edinburgh
Mrs. Baird, Edinburgh
Mrs. R. M. Baird, Edinburgh
Mrs. Harold R. Becker, Cupar
Mrs. P. Begg, Farnham
Serge Belossesky, Ipswich, Mass., U.S.A.
Anthony Besch, London
M. Brebner, Aberdeen
Messrs. Blacklock, Farries & Sons, Ltd., Dumfries
Blackwell's Exports, Oxford
Mrs. Andrew Bogdan, Scarborough
Miss Eila Bonthrone, Elgin
Robert W. Borland, S.S.C., Edinburgh
Bournemouth Municipal Libraries
Museum of Fine Arts, Boston, 15, U.S.A.
The Rt. Hon. The Earl of Bradford, Shropshire
Miss Edyth Bray, Guelph, Canada
Mrs. Harrison G. Bridge, Chestnut Hill, Mass., U.S.A.
Brighton Public Library
Mrs. Charles H. Brown, Lake Forest, Illinois, U.S.A.
The Hon. Mrs. James Bruce, Balmanno Castle.
Bruntons of George Street Ltd., Edinburgh
His Grace the Duke of Buccleuch and Queensberry, K.T., G.C.V.O., Drumlanrig Castle.
Her Grace the Duchess of Buccleuch and Queensbury, Drumlanrig Castle
James H. Buchan, Fairfax, Virginia, U.S.A.
Sir J. W. Buchanan-Jardine, Bt., Castle Milk
Mrs. P. H. Budden, Rochester
Messrs. J. & E. Bumpus Ltd., London
Mrs. Robert M. Bunzl, Atlanta, Ga., U.S.A.
Mrs. Aline Burn-Murdoch, Edinburgh
The Most Hon. The Marquess of Bute, Mount Stuart, Isle of Bute
P. Cairns, Durham
Miss Jean C. Campbell, Edinburgh
Mrs. Tucker Carrington, Richmond, Virginia, U.S.A.
Dr. & Mrs. Hoyle Campbell, Toronto, Canada
Carlisle Public Libraries
Mrs. Jack Case, New York, U.S.A.
Cumberland County Library
Countess Cawdor, Cawdor Castle
The Promenade Bookshop, Cheltenham
John Chiene, C.A., T.D., O.B.E., Edinburgh
Mrs. J. B. W. Christie, Monifieth
Robert Benjamin Church, Jr., Atlanta, Georgia, U.S.A.
Florence E. Cooke, La Jolla, California, U.S.A.
Mrs. J. J. Cochrane, Edinburgh
Mr. & Mrs. Gerret Copeland, N.Y., U.S.A.
Elizabeth P. Corning, Albany, N.Y., U.S.A.
Cornwall County Library
Mrs. & Miss Couper, Inverness
Miss Cowan Douglas, Kelso
The Rt. Hon. the Earl of Crawford and Balcarres, K.T., G.B.E., Balcarres
Mrs. A. H. Crerar, Edinburgh
C. C. Cumming, Edinburgh Pictorial Ltd.
Miss M. L. Dalgleish, M.A., Edinburgh
Carnegie Public Library, Coatbridge
Francis James Dallett, Tellisford, near Bath
Miss H. M. Dickson, Duns
Mrs. J. H. Dickson, Nassau, Bahamas

Professor Gordon Donaldson, Edinburgh
Dring's Bookshop, Newcastle-on-Tyne
Elizabeth C. Dudley, Albany, N.Y., U.S.A.
J. G. Dunbar, Edinburgh
Mrs. Paul Du Vivier, American Consulate, Edinburgh
Dorothy East, San Diego, U.S.A.
Edinburgh Public Libraries
Edinburgh College of Art
Edinburgh Architectural Association
Professor and Mrs. Howard M. Ehrmann, Ann Arbor, Michigan, U.S.A.
Mrs. Sally Sample Ely, Princeton, New Jersey, U.S.A.
Mrs. Elwyn Evans, Greenville, Delaware, U.S.A.
Nicholas Fairbairn, Fordell Castle, Dunfermline
Falkirk Public Library
Mrs. E. Farfan, Pittenweem
Mrs. Helen Ferguson, Aberdeen
Miss J. P. S. Ferguson, Edinburgh
Mrs. Phyllis C. Ferry, La Jolla, Calif., U.S.A.
Hubert Fenwick, A.R.I.B.A., Edinburgh
Fife County Library
Mrs. Richard W. Finch, Colorado, U.S.A.
Mrs. M. E. Flanagan, Essex
Mrs. Flood, Salisbury
Mrs. F. G. Gallie, Edinburgh
Mr. William Cabell Garbee, Richmond, Virginia, U.S.A.
The Viscount Garnock, Yorkshire
Lt. Col. Gayre of Gayre and Nigg, Edinburgh
Paul E. Geier, Rome, Italy
Oliver A. Gill, California, U.S.A.
Gosforth Public Library
Messrs. Goulden & Curry, Ltd., Tunbridge Wells
Mrs. N. C. Graham, Edinburgh
Mrs. Grainger-Stewart, Edinburgh
Sir Francis C. Grant, Bt., Monymusk
Mrs. H. M. Grant, Coupar Angus
Dr. & Mrs. Robert W. Greenleaf, Indianapolis, U.S.A.
Mrs. George C. Gregory, Richmond, Virginia, U.S.A.
Mrs. Robert Guest, Toronto, Canada
Roger and Doris Habert, Watertown, Mass., U.S.A.
Robert Campbell Hadley, Denver, U.S.A.
Dr. I. Simson Hall, Edinburgh
His Grace the Duke of Hamilton, Lennoxlove
Mrs. J. Hanchet-Taylor, Aberfeldy
Brigadier Gen. H. D. Hansen, U.S.M.C. (Ret), Philadelphia, U.S.A.
Harvard College Library, Cambridge, Mass., U.S.A.
W. C. Henderson & Sons, Ltd., University Press, St. Andrews
Dr. L. W. Hereward, Dorchester
Mrs. Eleanor Henderson Herl, Silver-Spring, Md., U.S.A.
Herschel Gower, Nashville, Tennessee, U.S.A.
Lady Hesketh, Towcester
Mrs. George Heyneman, San Diego, California, U.S.A.
Miss J. Hilson, Cirencester
Miss Dorothy H. Hinnitt, New York, U.S.A.
A. M. Hodge, Edinburgh
John B. Hollister, Cincinnati, Ohio, U.S.A.
The Holt-Jackson Book Company, Ltd., Lytham St. Annes
Messrs. W. & R. Holmes (Books) Ltd., Glasgow
Lady Bridget Douglas Home, Coldstream
Lady Douglas Home, Coldstream
Mrs. Hope, Luffness
Mrs. George S. Howell, Eatontown, New Jersey, U.S.A.
Miss B. R. Howie, Cheltenham
Hudsons Bookshops Ltd., Birmingham
Edith M. B. Hughes, A.R.I.B.A., F.R.I.A.S., Edinburgh
Col. R. L. Hunter, Edinburgh
Henry E. Huntington Library and Art Gallery, California, U.S.A.
The Lady Inchyra, Inchyra House, Glencarse
Indiana University Library, U.S.A.
Miss C. Inglis, Craigrothie
M. R. Innes of Edingight, Edinburgh
Inverness Public Library & Museum
Irish Methodist Publishing Co. Ltd., Belfast
H. Q. Forbes Irvine, Drum Castle
Mrs. Quentin Irvine, Barra Castle
Major Francis Irvine, Straloch
Jackson's Library Service Ltd., Southport
Francis Johnson, J.P., F.S.A., Bridlington
Mrs. M. L. Johnson, West Newton, Mass., U.S.A.
Walter E. Johnson, Tamworth, U.S.A.
Mrs. R. D. G. Johnston, Ayrshire
Joint Universities Libraries, Nashville, Tennessee, U.S.A.

Miss Eileen C. Jordan, Edinburgh
Keighley Central Library
Miss M. Keith, Thurso
Moultrie R. Kelsall, Blairlogie
Mrs. M. Kennedy, Kippford
Central Public Library, Royal Borough of Kensington & Chelsea
Russell Kirk, Mecosta, Michigan, U.S.A.
Kirkcaldy Public Library
Mrs. N. Knoop, Jersey, Channel Islands
George H. Lawrence, Edinburgh
Mrs. Edward L. Leahy, Bristol, R.I., U.S.A.
The Hon. John W. Leslie, Brechin
Mrs. Bertha Liddell, Pitlochry
Dr. Robert A. Lillie, O.B.E., Edinburgh
Mrs. Jean Blair Lovell, Worthing
Miss Helen M. Lowe, Edinburgh
Mrs. Mary O. H. Luciani, Aboyne
James C. Luke, Inverness
Mrs. Charles J. Lynn, Indianapolis, Indiana, U.S.A.
Donald P. McAlpine, Edinburgh
Dr. M. S. McCready, Guelph, Canada
Macdonald Institute, University of Guelph, Ontario, Canada
Sheriff Alistair MacDonald, Lerwick
Macdonald College Library, Province of Quebec, Canada
Messrs. McDougal Brothers, Paisley
Sir Compton Mackenzie, Edinburgh
C. H. Mackenzie, Kyleakin, Isle of Skye
Mrs. Barbara Mackie, Bournemouth
Mrs. I. J. Mackinlay, Calvine
Macmillan's Bookshop, St. Andrews
Mrs. Anne MacNaughton, Lochearnhead
Mrs. McMurtrie, Balbithan
J. H. McNeil, Nassau, Bahamas
Dr. & Mrs. Colin MacRae, Alexandria, Virginia, U.S.A.
Dr. & Mrs. Colin McRae, Toronto, Canada
Right Rev. Monsignor David McRoberts, Carstairs
Maidenhead Public Library
Mrs Paul B. Magnuson, Washington, D.C., U.S.A.
Dr. F. William Marlow, Jr., M.D., Brookline, Mass., U.S.A.
James I. H. Marshall, A.R.I.B.A., A.R.I.A.S., Edinburgh
Miss Margaret Marshall, Edinburgh
Robin M. Martin, Edinburgh
Massachusetts Horticultural Society Library, Boston, U.S.A.
Miss Gertrude Matheson, Edinburgh
Mrs. R. F. Matlat, W. Chester, Pa., U.S.A.
Miss A. C. Methven, Edinburgh
William N. Mewbourne, Atlanta, Georgia, U.S.A.
The University of Michigan, U.S.A.
Brigadier and Mrs. W. J. Miller, La Mesa, California, U.S.A.
J. M. Milne Esq., Aberdeen
University of Minnesota Libraries, U.S.A.
Mrs. A. H. Mitcalfe, Milton Brodie
Miss M. P. Montgomery, Kirkcudbright
Montrose Public Library
Robert Spottiswoode Morpeth, F.S.A. Scot., Edinburgh
Paul H. Morton, M.D., F.A.C.P., Coronado, Califonia, U.S.A.
Motherwell Library
Captain P. Munro of Foulis, Ardullie
Joseph A. Murray, Edinburgh
Lt. Col. J. K. R. Murray, Cheltenham
Maj.-Gen. D. M. Murray-Lyon, Pitlochry
Mrs. A. Douglas Myers, Seattle, U.S.A.
National Museum of Antiquities of Scotland
National Trust for Historic Preservation, Washington, D.C., U.S.A.
National Trust for Scotland
D. C. Neillands, Edinburgh
Miss C. P. Nicoll, Maidstone
Mrs. P. M. Badenach Nicolson, Glenbervie
John R. Noble, St. Andrews
Scott Noble, Washington, D.C., U.S.A.
Mrs. C. E. Norton, Virginia, U.S.A.
Mrs. Garrison Norton, Washington, D.C., U.S.A.
Donald A. Oliver, Solihull
Lady Ogilvy, Cortachy Castle
Oxfordshire County Library
Miss Kathleen Paisley, Edinburgh
D. B. Pattullo, Edinburgh
Ian N. Pattullo, Meigle
J. C. Pattullo, Edinburgh
Lieut-Col. & Mrs. J. D. Pattullo, Edinburgh
Mr. & Mrs. J. P. Pattullo, Edinburgh
Kenneth Pattullo, Edinburgh
Margaret Pattullo, Vancouver, Canada
Robert Pattullo, Edinburgh
Marion Pattullo, Portland, Ore., U.S.A.
Miss Mary M. Pattullo, Forfar
Mr. & Mrs. M. L. Pattullo, Lathrisk, Fife
Mrs. C. G. M. Pearson, Edinburgh

Pennsylvania Horticultural Society, U.S.A.
D. W. Pettigrew, Dalbeattie
Mrs. E. S. Phillips, Edinburgh
Dr. H. Pringle, Edinburgh
Dr. R. W. Pringle, Edinburgh
Robert Pringle, Edinburgh
Mrs. Rachel Purvis, Earlshall
Mrs. Bruce Rae, New York, U.S.A.
Mrs. F. G. Ratcliffe, Crail
Lady Reid, Haddington
Richmond Public Library, Virginia, U.S.A.
John Robertson, Edinburgh
Miss E. G. Robertson, Berwick-on-Tweed
Mr. & Mrs. John Rodger, Crieff
Miss E. Rose, Kilravock Castle
Sir Henry J. Ross, Edinburgh
Ross shire County Library
The Royal Highland & Agricultural Society of Scotland
Royal Institute of British Architects
Lady Russell, Edinburgh
Miss L. West Russell, London
Professor Charles Ryskamp, Princeton, New Jersey, U.S.A.
John Salmon, B.A., F.S.A., Wellington
St Andrews University Library
Major M. E. M. Sandys, Ulverston
Scarborough Public Library
Mrs. W. E. Schevill, Concord, Mass., U.S.A.
"The Scots Magazine"
Mrs. I. M. Scott, Camberley
Dr. J. Terrell Scott, San Diego, California, U.S.A.
Mrs. Schumacher, Edinburgh
Seafield Estates, Cullen
Miss Elizabeth Seton, London
Scottish Central Library
Robert Shadforth, London
Mrs. I. A. Shannon, London
Peter O. Sharp, Banff
Mrs. N. Melville Shepherd, Edinburgh
Mrs. C. M. Sherriff, Edinburgh
Society of Writers to H. M. Signet, Signet Library, Edinburgh
Mrs. Sillitto, Edinburgh
Dr. Grant G. Simpson, Edinburgh
Mrs. M. Simpson, Muchalls Castle
Basil C. Skinner, Edinburgh
Mrs. Mona Sleigh, Edinburgh
Mrs. M. I. Slessor, Inverness
Robert H. Sonnier, New York, U.S.A.
Rupert N. R. Smith,
John Smith & Son (Glasgow) Ltd., Glasgow
Staffordshire County Library
Mary Stanley-Smith, Oxford
Miss Nell A. Stearn, San Diego, California, U.S.A.
Mrs. H. L. Steel, Edinburgh
Mrs. W. E. Stephenson, Consett, Co. Durham
Miss Adèle M. Stewart, Edinburgh
Stirling County Library
Stirling Public Library
Miss M. P. Stout, Pulborough
Mrs. R. H. A. Swain, Edinburgh
Mrs. Henry Magruder Taylor Jr., Richmond, Virginia, U.S.A.
Mrs. Peter Tennant, Callander
Irene Buchan Thompson,
Lady Thomson, Forres
The Times Book Co., Ltd., London
The Rev. A. Stewart Todd, Edinburgh
Dr. T. R. R. Todd, Edinburgh
Dr. Ethlyn Trapp, Vancouver, Canada
Trust Company of South Carolina, U.S.A.
Madame B. Tessier, Nantes, France
John R. Upton, M.D., C.B.E., San Francisco, U.S.A.
Bruce Urquhart of Craigston, Craigston Castle
Mrs. Wm. H. Van Dusen, Southport, Connecticut, U.S.A.
W. Leicester Van Leer, New York, U.S.A.
Dorothy Van Nuys, Portland, Oregon, U.S.A.
Mrs. C. C. Vincent, Broadstairs
University of Virginia, the School of Architecture Library, U.S.A.
Virginia Museum of Fine Arts, U.S.A.
Mrs. M. G. Graham Wade, Broadway
Mrs. S. K. Wagner, Houston, Texas, U.S.A.
R. M. Webster, Banff
Mrs. Thomas E. West, Jr., Eaton, Ohio, U.S.A.
West Riding County Library
Mrs. W. A. Whitelaw, Cawdor
Alex D. Williams, Columbus, Ohio, U.S.A.
Colonial Williamsburg Department of Collections, Virginia, U.S.A.
Dr. Douglas Young, Tayport
Charles Wilson (Booksellers) Ltd., Liverpool
Guy Woolford, Tucson, Arizona, U.S.A.
The Woolston Book Co. Ltd., Nottingham
York City Libraries

Additional Subscribers

Mrs. Halstead T. Anderson, Macon Ga., U.S.A.
The British Bookshop, Hong Kong
Mrs. Charles P. Burgess, Washington, D.C. U.S.A.
E. Leslie Byrnes Jr., Lakeville, Conn., U.S.A.
Mrs. George Chiene, Edinburgh
The Cosmopolitan Club, New York, U.S.A.
Mrs. John H. Cunningham, Brookline, Mass., U.S.A.
John Cunningham, New York, U.S.A.
Donald Douglass, Sarasota, Fla., U.S.A.
Mrs. Claud E. Eley Jr., Kittanning, Pa., U.S.A.
Mrs. J. Fleischmann, Cincinnati, U.S.A.
Mrs. Mary Parvin Goodman, Morristown, N.J., U.S.A.
Robert Herman, New Rochelle, N.Y., U.S.A.
George Hogg, London
Donald Houghton, San Francisco, U.S.A.
Indianapolis Art Museum
Sinclair Jacobs, Atlanta, Ga., U.S.A.
Mrs. John Colgate Jessup, New York, U.S.A.
Mrs. Jean Drummond Jones, Ft., Atkinson, U.S.A.
William Kidd & Sons, Ltd., Dundee
William T. Leith, Washington, D.C., U.S.A.
Donald MacDonald D. Thurber, Groose Pointe, Mich., U.S.A.
James H. Macdonald, La Junta, Colo., U.S.A.
Lady Macleod, London
Malcolm Stuart McConihe Jr., Oyster Bay, N.Y., U.S.A.
Mrs. James W. McCook Jr., Macon, Ga., U.S.A.
Mrs. Helen Tytler Sunny McKibbin, Chicago, U.S.A.
Donald Moor Galleries Ltd., Hong Kong.
Mrs. Herman G. Place, New York, U.S.A.
Major Neil Ramsay, Aberfeldy
Thomas Rosswall, Lidingo, Sweden
Miss Lois West Russell, London
Sandeman Public Library, Perth
James M. Snitzler, Washington, D.C., U.S.A.

Mrs. B. Hoffstot, Palm Beach, U.S.A.
Shannon Pedlow, California, U.S.A.
Douglas C. Ross, Woodstock, U.S.A.
Miss Grace McNaughton, Balquhidder
Mrs. Jean Innes, Balquhidder
Mr. & Mrs. M. Beilby, Edinburgh
Mrs. Christopher R. Webster, Raleigh, N.C., U.S.A.
Mrs. Ena McMillan, Balmacara
University of Tennessee, Knoxville, U.S.A.

The American Museum in Britain. Bath
Waltraud Emmrich, Frankfurt, Germany
National Trust of Australia (Victoria)
Rodney Davidson, Toorak, Australia
Mrs. W. G. Robertson, Crail
Lt. Col. A. O. Dennistoun, Woking
Nordisk Boghandel, Copenhagen, Denmark
Miss Anne Macfarlane, J.P., Edinburgh
Dr. P. J. M. McEwan, Ballater

Notes

Notes

Notes